PICTURED
MEMORIES
OF
HUNTING

Margarita Chamberlayne

HALSGROVE

First edition published in Great Britain in 2000 by Nicky Greenwood
Second edition published in 2002 by Halsgrove

Copyright © 2000 Margarita Chamberlayne

British Library Cataloguing-in-Publication Data
A CIP record for this title is available from the British Library

ISBN 1 84114 169 0

HALSGROVE
Halsgrove House
Lower Moor Way
Tiverton, Devon EX16 6SS
Tel: 01884 243242
Fax: 01884 243325
email: sales@halsgrove.com
website: www.halsgrove.com

Printed and bound in Italy by Centro Grafico Ambrosiano.

Please note: In the 'Horses Out' column, 'D' stands for 'Daddy's Horse'.

PICTURED MEMORIES OF HUNTING

I am delighted to be able to write a foreword to this fascinating account of hunting life in the 1920's and 1930's by Margarita Chamberlayne. Margarita is a wonderful character, very energetic and outgoing with a keen sense of observation and humour which she brought to her writing and drawings and who lived in Steeple Aston with her father between the wars. She worked hard on many of the local farms helping out during the war. After the war she married Gregory Stapleton, who was in the Indian Army and spent time in Burma and India and latterly in Kenya at the time of the Mau Mau rebellions, before returning to England in the early fifties, when her husband was appointed Political Agent to the local MP, Lord Hitchinbrook, and moved to Dorset.

Her diaries provide a remarkable insight into hunting life and incidents at that period and are written in a lively and interesting way with a great sense of humour and with many delightful coloured illustrations which she did herself.

The reference to cousin Edward in the diaries is my Grandfather who was her cousin and who was living at Chipping Norton at the same time. It is marvellous to read her accounts of days with the Heythrop, Bicester and Warickshire Hounds in an area which is more difficult for hunting nowadays with the advent of motorways etc.

Born in 1908, she still lives in Dorset and is actively enjoying her garden.

Simon Chamberlayne
May 2000

AT THE MEET.

A Selection of Illustrations from

Margarita Chamberlayne's Hunting Journal

3

HORSES OUT
Dinah; D. Redfern

WELL JUMPED SIR!

Rather cold and high wind. Sunny morning. We arrived just as they killed the second fox in the laurels. This was all Major Daly had come to do, but however, we drew Dane Hill and a fox ran back towards N.Aston and then turned towards the Oxford road and was lost. Then we drew the osier beds along the river and Middle Aston and the warren all blank. Duns Tew Gorse held a fox and he ran nearly to Hempton and was lost. Then, after drawing a double hedgerow blank hounds went home.

I saw one poor man, whose horse jumped big over a little fence, jumped clean off! He has my deepest sympathy. A boy on a rough pony pushed its head under cousin Edwards arm, just as a crowd was scrambling through the little gate over the bridge, whereupon cousin Edward clenched his fist and hammered the pony's nose. Both the boy and the pony were very little abashed! Uncle Frank out looking very run down after his flu. Young Mrs Daly swam in the brook - she must have had a cold ride home.

HORSES OUT
Redfern; D.John D.

THE FIRST IS LAST.

Sunny in morning, became stormy and dark. They found in Poodle Gorse, ran through Fringford Hill and went left handed past Cotmore House and the kennels, back to Poodle Gorse. Continuing over Pounden Hill and past Twyford to Three Bridge Mill, they turned right handed past Portway Gorse to Charndon Wood, where we left them. A good slow hunt with very bad scent. We had 18 long miles home. John D. very slow today but Redfern very keen and jumped very well.

HORSES OUT
Dinah; D. Eldridge

TWO OPINIONS.

They drew Fritwell Gorse blank, and killed one at once in Poor's Piece. A fox was found in Stoke Big Wood and ran slowly for a few fields - scent very poor. Hounds went home at 2.30 after drawing Grunthill blank.

Eldridge very excited and enjoying his first day immensely. Dinah jumping well except some wattle hurdles that she hates, and which she refused twice, but came over the third time! Maureen Waldron out on an old hireling. Wet ride home only luckily short.

THE MASTER LEADS THE FIELD.

HORSES OUT
Dinah; D.John D.

Cloudy and mild, wind and rain in the afternoon. Everywhere was blank till we came to Churchill Heath, where a fox broke and ran for a couple of fields, but was headed back from the road, back to the cover. He broke again the other side but after two fields he got to ground under an oak tree in a meadow. A fox was found in the Norrells and after running a few fields he too returned to cover and we left them as we were a long way from home. John D. went much better than usual. Dinah very fresh. Only one fence to jump today. Lots of children and ponies out. Came back part of the way with Mr Nutting, Allpey and Col. Ballard.

HORSES OUT
Eldridge; D.Redrern

DEEP going.

Cold and very dark at first but became warmer and lighter. They drew New Cover, Graven Hill and Arncott Wood and ran past Whitecross Green to Shabbington Woods and there we lost them. They ran fast, but the going was terribly deep and boggy up to a horse's hocks. Once in Shabbington Woods it was impossible to keep near them so we came home. 20 miles home! A long ride home and dark when we arrived. My first hunt on Eldridge this year. He went so gallantly and was very excited.

HORSES OUT
Dinah; D. John D.

" GONE TO GROUND! NOW WE CAN GO HOME! "

Very cold, thin wetting rain all day. We rode to the meet, but were a little late and found them just going to draw Railway Cover. A fox ran across the railway, over a few meadows, back across the line and was lost before crossing the road from Nell Bridge. We jogged all along the main road to Deddington, drawing a field of roots blank on our way. We then turned down the bridle road to North Aston and a fox was found in some gorse close by. He ran downhill, over the brook, along the other side, back again across it and was lost. Dane Hill and North Aston were drawn blank. An outlier was found in a meadow off the Duns Tew - Barton road and ran up close to Brasenose Farm and was lost near Barton bushes. Seagrove Osiers produced a fox who ran to Worton heath and there got to ground. Hounds ran very fast when they did run, but not for long.

HORSES
Eldridge; D. Redfren

GONE TO GROUND.

Mild. South wind becoming stronger in afternoon. Few drops of rain. Chalton Spinney and Thomas' Gorse were blank. A fox ran from Northcote Hill nearly to Newbottle and back again and got to ground in the old Roman Camp. Then the Pest House wood, Aynhoe Park and Croughton Bottom and Tusmore were drawn blank. A fox came away from Stoke Bushes, and ran down nearly to Hethe Brede, back to Tusmore, away to Cottisford to Shelswell Plantation and on towards Spilsmere Wood, where we had to leave them. Very large field out. Eldridge went so well. He did hit the binder in one very tall fence, very hard and pecked rather badly, and I came off, but as Dunning says, better that than to stay on the wrong side. Aunt Daisy out, and Uncle John. Several men lost their hats in Tusmore Wood, under the yew trees which grow very low. One poor man whose horse hit a rail in a fence surrounded by flood water, was pressed in the mud and got up as black as a chimney sweep!

HORSES OUT
Dinah; D. John D

THE ADMIRAL SUPERINTENDS HOUNDS WHILE DRAWING BIGNELL

Mild in morning - very cold and showers of hail in afternoon. We drew Busby's Spinney blank and then back to the village and bolted a fox from a stick heap. He ran nearly to Hampton Poyle and back again into Kirtlington Park and was lost. Kirtlington Roundabouts were then drawn blank and at last a fox was found and ran to Trow Pool and back near to Middleton Village and back to Bignell Park. He was holloa'd by a shepherd up on the higher ground and hounds hunted him back to Middleton and lost him in Trow Pool. Not a big field out. Our horses went well. Old Admiral Ruck-Keane very pleased at having a fox at Bignell.

DINAH JUMPS THE BROOK.

Very cold - rained all day. When we moved off we drew some little bits of gorse below Hinton and then Gooseholme, all blank, but a fox came from Brackley Gorse and ran to Colready, where there was a long check, but he ran on to Farthinghoe, down past Owen Cole's farm, over the brook, past Farthinghoe Station to Cockley Brake, then left handed to Thenford and he got to ground in a hedgerow between Middleton Cheney and Purston. We came home then. Great run, very fast. Dinah jumped the brook, many people got in. Very wet coming home.

DADDY AND REDFERN.

HORSES OUT
Eldridge. D. Redfern

Mild and cloudy - rained heavily till 11 o'clock. Sunny late. Prattle Wood was drawn first and was blank. Then we went down in the low meadows below Prattle Wood to draw a stick heap which was blank. Then went on nearly to Oddington, drawing another stick heap blank, but at Oddington stick heap a fox came out and turned back into it but another came out and ran past Weston Wood to Wormough where he was killed. A piece of gorse was then drawn and a fox was killed almost at once. Then we went on up to Weston Aerodrome and a fox was found in a rushy meadow there and ran in a circle through Wendlebury, back near the aerodrome, through Wendlebury again and was lost near where we found him. Lots of jumping - Eldridge went so well. Only about 50 people out.

DADDY COMES DOWN AT THE BROOK.

HORSES OUT
Dinah; D. Redfern

Bitterly cold - snowstorms and hail. A fox came away from Rignell, but after running a few fields towards South Newington he was lost. One from Millington's Gorse ran over the hill towards Hempton then left handed close by Great Tew and Sandford Park and he was lost in Conygree. A blizzard was blowing when we drew Worton Heath, but as soon as the snow stopped a fox ran away left handed from the top of the cover towards Barton, then right handed through Sandford Park to Conygree where they checked, on near Over Worton and lost him a few fields from Worton Heath. Dinah went well. Good going, good hunt and big fences.

GONE TO GROUND.

DADDY AND REDFERN REST AWHILE.

HORSES OUT
Eldridge; D. Redfern

Warm in the morning - cloudy and colder later. We rode on to the meet, and they were drawing Enstone Plantation when we arrived, but it was blank and they went on to Henley Knapp, where a fox ran fast across three ploughed fields into Shilston Wood and across Ditchley Park and was lost. A fox was found in Dog Kennel Wood, but nothing was done with him. After running round for a long time in cover, a fox went from Sheers Copse into Ditchley Park and got to ground. Hill Woods etc. and Swan's Nest were all drawn blank. No sport, but quite a nice ride all about Ditchley. Eldridge very fresh.

UNCLE FRANK TEACHES A YOUNG 'UN TO GO.

Warm and dull. We went straight to Worton Heath and got there about 8.45 to find them still drawing. About three cubs there but none killed. Seagrove Osiers held at least one but he was lost. There were several in Duns Tew Gorse and one went away back to Worton Heath and then turned east, but the going was too hard to gallop and we could not keep up. Uncle Frank was out. D. liked Hillmorton. We popped over a low rail and a broken gate. So lovely to begin hunting again.

NOT QUITE JUMPED OFF!

(MYSELF AND DINAH).

HORSES OUT
Dinah. D. Redfern

Bright and mild - strong gale. We were late for the meet, but arrived at the cover beyond Hook Norton just as the fox went away. He went away over a stiff line of country to within a mile of Swacliffe Common where was lost. Only Daddy, Col.Ballard and I were with hounds except for Lawrence and the 1st Whip. Then went on back to Hook Norton and found a fox in a kale field near Swerford and ran him to ground near the Mason's Arms. Frenches Hollow was blank but there were 2 at least in Hawk Hill. One went away and was lost after a few fields and then we came home. The horses jumped beautifully some big fence

LITTLE MISS HOLLAND HIBBERT IN DISTRESS.

HORSES OUT
Hillmorton.

Strong wind. Rain started as we came home and poured. Hunted today with the South Oxfordshire for the first time. First of all they drew all the rushy meadows and rough hedgerows down on Otmoor but they were all blank so they came up the hill and found a fox in Noke Wood. He kept running from wood to wood and there was very little scent among the bracken. After hunting him about for over an hour hounds lost him and went home. We didn't have much of a day but enjoyed seeing new country and a new pack. Everyone was very friendly and welcoming. Longish ride home in the wet.

AUNT DAISY MISBEHAVES.

HORSES OUT
Dinah; D. Hillmorton.

Still and cold, bright sun. Charlie took the horses on for me. Cockley Brake was drawn first and there were two cubs there. One got to ground and while the hounds were hunting him still, the other got away. Then we drew Farthinghoe Lodge and at once a fox went away all through Colready to Rowlers where he was lost. Then we drew Charlton Spinney blank and Thomas's Gorse. Then we went to Gooseholme and a fox went away to Brackley gorse and back to Gooseholme and away to Colready, through the cover and was killed in a field of roots by the road from Charlton to Hinton. A good day and lots of galloping and jumping. The horses went very well. Huge field out.

ON THE WAY TO THE OPENING MEET,

HORSES OUT
Redfern. D. Barney.

Still and cloudy - rather cold. The opening meet and a big field. Dreadful lot of fresh kicking horses around. Drew Poodle Gorse first blank. A fox went away from Stratton Copse ran to Godington, over the hill and back again to Stratton Copse. He then did the same round again but was killed before reaching Stratton Copse again. Then they drew Brook Spinneys and a fox went away at once through Shelswell Park to Tusmore where he was killed. Hounds got onto another at once and followed him without stopping to break up the first fox and he was hunted to Stoke Bushes across the road and was killed in some farm buildings.

A BLIND DITCH IS "A WERRY NASTY PLACE!"

HORSES OUT
Barney; D.Eldridge

Warm and dull. Emberlin's kale provided two foxes. One went to ground after two fields and the other was killed after two fields. An outlier was found in Croxton's Gorse and hunted to Middleton Ridings and lost. A fox was found in Letchmere Gorse and ran to Ballard's firs and got into a drain near the aerodrome. He was bolted and ran in Letchmere Gorse where he was killed. Trow Pool was blank but a fox came away from Grunthill and ran towards Bucknell and back overe the railway to Trow Pool and was lost.

COUSIN EDWARD GETS A NASTY FALL FROM A BLIND DITCH

HORSES OUT
Dinah. D. Redfern.

Warm and sunny. We joined the hounds as they were drawing Millington's Gorse and went on with them to Dean Hill. A fox ran from there towards North Aston, turned back over the brook and ran to the Deddington - Clifton road and back again to Millington's Gorse, over the same ground back to Deddington and was killed in Millington's Gorse. A fox went away from North Aston, crossed river, canal and railway and was lost between Somerton and Souldern. Very fast hunt. First time we have ever seen a fox cross the river. Cousin Edward and Col.Maclean had nasty falls. Col. Maclean died the day after.

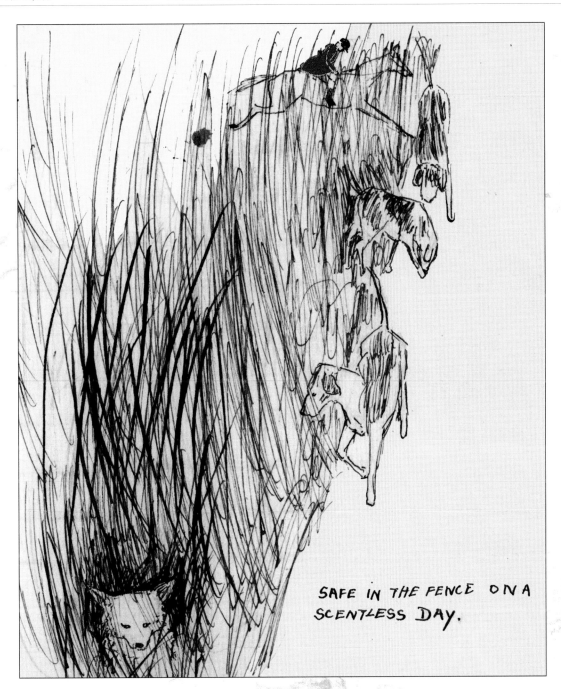

SAFE IN THE FENCE ON A
SCENTLESS DAY.

HORSES OUT
Eldridge. D. Barney

Bright sun and mild. From Busby Spinney hounds ran to below Kirtlington and back leaving Bletchington on the left and lost their fox near Harris Gorse. An outlier which they found then, ran past Heathfield and Weston Village and leaving Weston Wood on their left lost him at Oddington Siding. From Hayne's stick heap they ran through Charlton and we left them then. Scent improved wonderfully in the afternoon. The horses went so well. Very enjoyable day - lots of jumping and a smaller field than usual.

A SAD LOOK-OUT FOR THE BOWLER.

HORSES OUT
Dinah; D. Redfern;
Eldridge

Very strong gale - threatened rain but none fell. Glympton Heath was drawn blank. A fox came away from Tinford Gorse and ran along the green lane to Barton Lodge and back to Glympton Heath, where he was lost. A fox was found in Barton Osiers and ran west and then east again towards Tinford Bridge and was lost. Barton Mines and Barton Bushes were drawn blank, A fox came away from the Dean, crossed the Oxford road, ran past the Abbey towards Barton Bushes, then turned left handed to Seagrove Osiers where hounds gave up and went home as he was a long way ahead. Dinah jumped beautifully and was at her best today.

MRS. SULLIVAN
DONKEY STRAYS.

HORSES OUT
Eldridge; D. Redfern

Bright, cold and sunny - cold wind. They drew Hawk Hill first and a fox ran towards Nether Worton, past Mr Mitting's, to Ilbury Hill and back to Hawk Hill; he ran on again but was lost after a few fields. There was a fox at Rignell but got to ground at once. Millington's Gorse was blank but a fox went away from Duns Tew Gorse along the brook, over the turnpike nearly to Dane Hill and back nearly to Hempton and back to Duns Tew Gorse and was lost. Hounds then went to Seagrove Osiers, but Eldridge was so lame I took him home.

WE COME HOME THRO' BLENHEIM PARK.

HORSES OUT
Dinah; D. Barney

Dark, little wind, rather cold. The hounds found at Hanleys Copse and ran backwards and forwards between there and Dean Grove for some time and lost him. Henley Nap was blank, but a fox went away from Shilcott Wood and ran fast through Ditchley Park to Outwood where hounds were stopped because of shooting. After a long time a fox went from Sheer's Copse to Blenheim Park and as no one could follow the hounds over the park walls, by the time a gate was reached the fox was lost.

HORSES OUT
Barney. D.Redfern

MARIGOLD AND I WERE SUCCESSFUL IN OUR EFFORTS TO INDUCE THIS HORSE TO SAVE ITSELF

Mild, still and a little misty. They found a fox in Middleton Park and ran nearly to Northbrook, back to Middleton and on to Kirtlington Park and Bletchington village, back through Kirtlington Park, through Middleton Park to Trow Pool, then to Bignell where they killed him. Then they found an outlier in some roots near Chesterton but we left them there. Barney fell over the first fence, an oak style, but jumped very well all day after. Redfern came down with Daddy cantering down hill.

ONE HOUND BREAKS AWAY TO HER FORMER MISTRESS.

HORSES OUT
Dinah; D. Hillmorton

Bitterly cold and dark, sleet and rain. They met today instead of yesterday because of frost. It snowed over night but thawed in time for the meet. Very small field. They drew Mixbury Plantation first and a fox ran there through Finmere Plantation to Tingewick Wood where he was lost. A fox was found in the Round Wood but could only run a field or so. Long jog back to Stratton Copse where two foxes were found. One was chopped and the other ran out past Godington so we came home, Good day, Dinah jumped beautifully.

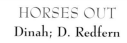

MASTER RUCKKEENE'S PONY TAKES CONTROL.

Very foggy and still. Hounds met today instead of yesterday on account of fog. Found in Weston Peat Pits and ran with Weston Aerodrome on right to Middleton Park and lost. Found a fox up a tree in Kirtlington and killed him at once. Found another up a tree and hunted him nearly to the Three Pigeons, then left handed to Hampton Gay, thru' Busby's Spinney and killed in Kirtlington Park.

THE SECOND WHIP

IN DIFFICULTY.

HORSES OUT
Barney; D. Hillmorton

Mild and cloudy - slightly windy. We met hounds near the water tower. They went straight to Cotmore Cover and found a fox who was killed short of Stratton Audley. Found next in Bainton Osiers and hunted slowly to Stoke Little Wood, back to Bainton, left handed back to Stoke Wood, then going away faster ran with Ardley on right to Trow Pool and on to Bicester Water Tower where fox was coursed by greyhound, then right handed to Bignell and killed. Drew Bucknell Spinney blank and we came home.

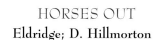

HORSES OUT
Eldridge; D. Hillmorton

WHAT THE ———— ARE YOU DOING MADAM ?

Slight wind, rained early and in afternoon - mild. Enormous field. A fox ran from Poodle Gorse to Stratton Copse, over Fringford Hill, through Cotmore, where there was a check, on by Bucknell to Trow Pool, into Middleton Stoney village and back to Trow Pool, where he got to ground. Fine hunt, fast and lots of jumping. Changed foxes at Cotmore. Very deep on the ploughs. Eldridge went so well.

THE MASTER'S HORSES ARRIVE FRESH.

HORSES OUT
Barney; D.Redfern

Cloudy, not much wind, cold. Hounds found at Fritwell Gorse and ran to Stoke Wood, through Bullock Pits, past Caversfield House, on by Cotmore to Bainton, back to Cotmore and near Braishfield House where he got to ground under the main road. A fox from Hethe Brede ran thru' Cotmore, by Caversfield House, on by Bullock Pits and Bucknell Spinney to Stoke Wood and on towards Stoke Bushes where we came home. Very good day - Barney went beautifully.

HORSES OUT
Dinah; D.Hillmorton

THE LEATHER BOTTLE.

MR. NUTTING PAUSES ON THE WAY HOME.

Cool and dark - rained softly all day. Holly Grove was blank. A fox was found in some gorse and ran into to Wychwood Forest, where he was hunted about and lost. Then Singe Wood and Job's Copse were drawn blank, but a fox from Cogge's Wood ran pointing for Wilcote, but was headed and turned right handed thru' Eynsham Park where they were still hunting him when we left. Long ride home. Nice little run at the end.

EMBERLIN'S KALE WAS

NOT BLANK.

HORSES OUT
Barney; D. Hillmorton

Warm and sunny turning cloudy later. We went early to the meet and had to wait an hour. Emberlin's kale was blank except for a puss. Ballard's Firs and Dog Kennel Spinney were blank. A fox was chopped in Stoke Wood. A fox ran from Stoke Bushes into Tusmore Park and round by the park and Hardwick Heath and we came home then. Lovely to be out at last after the frost. Just as well there was no jumping as the ground was still unfit.

HORSES OUT
Dinah; D. Redfern

GOING — GOING — G—

Misty in morning - very cold - cloudy all day. Found at Highland's Gorse and hunted with Broughton Castle on right in a left handed ring, back to Lower Tadmarton and lost. Found again at Highland's Gorse and ran past Broughton Castle to Claydon Hill Wood and lost. Got an outlier near Swacliffe but could do little.

IN THE HUNTING FIELD ALL ARE EQUALS.

HORSES OUT
Barney; D. Hillmorton

Cold and cloudy - cleared in afternoon. Huge field and lots of kicking horses. A fox from Keeper's Spinney seemed to run back to Thenford Gorse but was apparently lost. A fox from Cockley Brake , after hounds had chopped one in cover, ran towards Steane, then back to Farthinghoe Lodge, through Rosamond's Bower, checked in Wellifer, over the brook and railway, back over the railway leaving Purston on the right and up to Farthinghoe Lodge where we left them. Very nice hunt - Barney jumping beautifully.

DADDY ABANDONED ON THE SHORE.

HORSES OUT
Eldridge; D. Redfern

Very warm and sunny. Found near Longlands and ran well for first mile with kennels on right then very slowly left handed past Caversfield and Bullocks Pits by Gilbey's house over G.W.R., and past Bicester Workhouse and lost short of Bignell.

HORSES OUT
Dinah; D. Hillmorton

ARTHER DILLON ON HIS WAY TO THE MEET.

Warm and sunny. Found at Glympton Heath, ran towards Barton then turned back to Glympton Heath and was lost. Found in Tinford Gorse and ran to Wootton and on to nearly Glympton and lost. Drew Barton Mines, Round Wood and Bushes blank. An outlier jumped up between Barton and Duns Tew and ran pointed for Worton Heath but turned back, crossed the Oxford road and got to ground near Middle Aston. Found at Worton Heath, ran to Over Worton and we left them there.

ONE HOUND WAS KILLED.

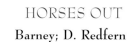

HORSES OUT
Barney; D. Redfern

Mild and sunny. Found in Hayne's stick heap and ran over railway, where one hound was killed by a train, back over the railway with Oddington on the left onto Otmoor, left handed with Charlton on the right to Wormough and Weston Wood and Charlton and lost near Merton - good hunt and fast. Found next at Ambrosden New Cover and lost at Ambrosden village. Found at Graven Hill and marked to ground under a tree near Merton.

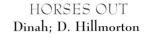

HORSES OUT
Dinah; D. Hillmorton

THE FOX REFUSED TO BE HEADED AWAY FROM HIS HOLE.

Very strong gale - cold. Found at Swerford Corner and ran to Mason's Arms cover and killed one and marked one to ground. Found at Rignell and hunted slowly to railway between Bloxham and Milcombe and lost. Hawk Hill was blank. Found at Great Tew and ran round the park and lost between there and Ledwell.

MRS. DILLON AND PEGGY RETURN IN LUXURY.

HORSES OUT
Barney

Cold and a breeze. Brook's Spinneys were blank, but a fox from Spilsbury ran to Chetwode and was killed. An outlier near Stratton Copse was hunted very slowly To Hethe Brede and lost. A fox from Longlands crossed the Bicester road and ran to Graven Hill where he was killed.

REFRESHMENTS FROM Mᴿ AND Mᴿˢ JUDGE.

HORSES OUT
Barney; D. Hillmorton

Sunny - very chill wind. Found at Colready and ran through Farthinghoe towards the station and back to Cockley Brake and killed there. Then they drew Keeper's Spinney and ran to Sulgrave and killed in a cottage garden. They then went to Thorpe Manderville to draw, but we came home. Ground very hard and very little jumping.

MRS. DALY HEADS BACK A CUB.

HORSES OUT
Dinah; D. Frank;
Gilbert. Hillmorton

Still and foggy early - rain later.
There were either one or two foxes in
the Dean; I think only one. He was
hunted about for 1½ hours and then
all trace of him was lost. Three cubs
ran from Daffodil Clump into
Haydon and four ran back to
Daffodil Clump. One was hunted
about Haydon for some time and
then got to ground in a rabbit hole
under a tree. The others had all gone
to ground in Daffodil Clump and two
were dug out and killed.

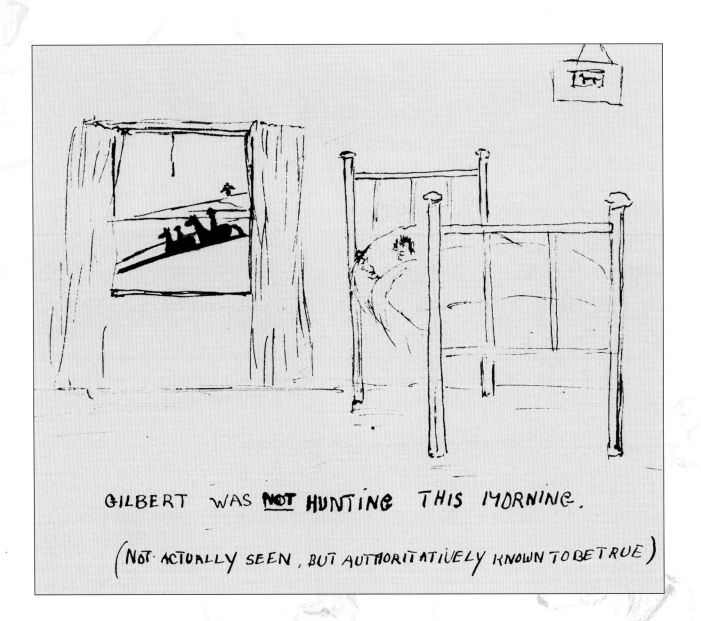

GILBERT WAS NOT HUNTING THIS MORNING.

(NOT ACTUALLY SEEN, BUT AUTHORITATIVELY KNOWN TO BE TRUE)

Fine and still - thick fog in the valley - rained all afternoon. We went late and hounds had already killed a fox in Cox's Spinney when we found them near the 'drome. Down's Spinney and Northbrook were blank and they hunted a fox well about Middleton Park and killed him. Then they found Trow Pool blank and went home.

HORSES OUT
Barney

BARNEY AND I COME IN FOR A STORM OF ABUSE FROM MRS. KIETH-FALCONER.

Cold and rained most of the day - warmer after noon. Prattle Wood was blank. Then we found a fox in a double hedge near Noke and ran with Log Farm on right to Oddington Halt - back left handed past Hayne's stick heap with Islip on right to Prattle Wood and on nearly to Noke Wood and lost. Found at Hayne's stick heap and ran with Log Farm on left to Noke Wood and back to Log Farm and killed.

HORSES OUT
Barney; D. Hillmorton

THE FIRST GATE-WAY AT THE OPENING MEET.

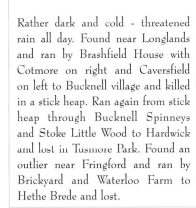

Rather dark and cold - threatened rain all day. Found near Longlands and ran by Brashfield House with Cotmore on right and Caversfield on left to Bucknell village and killed in a stick heap. Ran again from stick heap through Bucknell Spinneys and Stoke Little Wood to Hardwick and lost in Tusmore Park. Found an outlier near Fringford and ran by Brickyard and Waterloo Farm to Hethe Brede and lost.

MRS. DILLON IN THE OXFORD ROAD.

HORSES OUT
Barney; D.Hillmorton

Bright, clear and frosty. Found at Deddington Mill and ran up valley leaving Barford on right over Steepness Hill to Hawk Hill with Nether Worton on left up to Over Worton - left handed over Hempton - Duns Tew road over brook and to ground in Millington's gorse bushes. Did little at Rignell with 2 or 3 foxes. Found in Iron Down Gorse and ran a nice ring over Deddington - Chipping Norton road and back again and lost at Buttermilk.

MISS GOLD JOINS THE AIR CORPS.

HORSES OUT
Barney; D. Redfern

Cold and stormy. A fox was found in the Dean Plantation but was headed back into it again and lost. One from Daffodil Clump ran nearly to Sirett's farm and got to ground. (very mangy). Another from Daffodil Clump ran to the badger earths between North Aston and Somerton and got to ground. The Warren was blank. A fox from Dane Hill ran up to North Aston, on to the warren, over the Duns Tew road nearly to Deddington, crossed the main road again and ran back to Dane Hill and got to ground. Before this an earlier fox from Dane Hill ran nearly to Clifton and got to ground. Two foxes were chopped. One by Bowman's Bridge and one in North Aston Osiers. Last run was good fun.

MR GILBEY CONTINUED THIS HUNT ON FOOT.

HORSES OUT
Barney; D. Hillmorton

Very wet and windy. Found at
Busby's Spinney and ran to ground
in wood yard in Bletchington. Found
in Peat Pits ran round Kirtlington
Park and killed. Found an outlier in
Park and ran nearly to Baker's Copse
and lost.

HORSES OUT
Barney; D. Hillmorton

BARNEY AND I FORDING A BROOK.

Mild. Prattle Wood was blank. A fox from Hayne's stick heap ran with Charlton on right to Otmore and slowly hunted for 1½ hours till they lost at Log Farm. Found at Weston Wood and ran over L.M.S. railway and back with Wormough on left to Bignell and then came home.

EVEN SHIRE HORSES LIKE HUNTING.

HORSES OUT
Barney; D. Frank

Lovely and warm - just like a spring day. We got to the meet late because of a tyre bursting, but caught them up in Cogges Wood where they found and ran for an hour in Eynsham Park and lost. Found at the Hayes and ran thru" Ramsden village, Singe Wood and nearly to Leafield before running into Wychwood Forest where hounds were stopped.

51

HORSES OUT
Dinah; D. Redfern

WE COME HOME DEJECTEDLY.

Driving wind and rain all day. Rode to meet - wet through before arriving. Chopped a fox in Broadstone Hill. Lidstone Bottom blank. Found in Enstone Drive Plantation and ran by Lidstone Bottom and Broadstone Hill and lost. Came home.

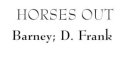

HORSES OUT
Barney; D. Frank

JUST BEFORE THE KILL

Windy and fine. Found in the Caudle and ran across the park to Kirtlington Roundabouts past Slade Farm and into Middleton Park and the Home Wood and killed near the house. After Lazarus Bottom and Weston Peat Pits blank, they found in a rough meadow near Wendlebury and ran pointing for Bignell, left handed to Weston Aerodrome and left again leaving Weston Wood and Wendlebury on right to Bignell and killed. Very nice hunt.

SOME ENJOYED HAT HUNTING AS WELL AS FOX-HUNTING.

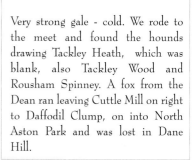

HORSES OUT
Barney; D. Redfern

Very strong gale - cold. We rode to the meet and found the hounds drawing Tackley Heath, which was blank, also Tackley Wood and Rousham Spinney. A fox from the Dean ran leaving Cuttle Mill on right to Daffodil Clump, on into North Aston Park and was lost in Dane Hill.

HORSES OUT
Dinah; D. Hillmorton

THIS BULLOCK THOUGHT IT WAS THE QUARRY.

Fine and sunny. All Aynhoe Covers were blank. Found at Rowlers and ran with Charlton on left to Colready, away pointing for Hinton and turned right handed and lost near Charlton.

HORSES OUT
Barney; D.Frank

PRIVATE DOGS ALSO ENJOYED THE BOXING DAY HUNT.

Fine and sunny. Found in Bullock's Pits and ran to ground at Bucknell. Found in Bucknell Spinney and killed at Swift's House. Found at Cotmore and ran by Bainton right handed back to Cotmore - away again by Bainton and we left them running slowly towards Stratton. Audley.

HORSES OUT
Barney; D. Redfern

IN DIFFICULTY, HAVING PRECEDED HIS HORSE OVER THE FENCE.

Found in Shelswell Plantation, through Finmere Plantation with Warren to left to Westbury Station, left handed to Mixbury Spinney and nearly to Finmere left handed over the Ouse with Shalstone on right and Westbury Weld on right to Turweston and lost. Found at Spilsmere, ran by Shelswell Plantation and lost at Cottisford. It would have been a good hunt if we could only have got over the river. Saw a farmer's horse die of paralysis while hunting.

THIS HORSE GOT A BAD OVER REACH HERE.

HORSES OUT
Barney

Bitterly cold - snow and rain nearly all day. Found at Wilcote and ran on beyond Ashford Mill, right handed nearly to Northleigh and back through Holly Grove to Wilcote very fast and then on very slowly to Charlbury and Stonesfield. Stonesfield Spinneys were blank so came home. Would have been a very good hunt if the country had been good. D. couldn't come as the other horses' backs were wrong.

HORSES OUT
Barney; D. Redfern

MRS. DILLON EXPOSTULATING IN 9 INCHES OF WATER.

Sunny and still - hazy later. Found in the Dean and ran along the foot path to flooded meadows below railway and killed. Daffodil Clump and Middle Aston blank. Dane Hill had a fox but the master wouldn't tell Laurence it had been seen. A fox from Duns Tew Gorse ran alongside the brook and got to ground on Ilbury Hill. A fox from Rignell ran through S. Newington Village and got to ground on S. Newington Hill. Good run . Found at Hawk Hill and ran to Worton and on to Hempton where we left them. Lovely day - great fun, nice country.

A STEEP HILLSIDE.

HORSES OUT
Redfern

Very warm - sunny and still. I rode on to the meet. They found in the Ovens and ran past Chapel House and got to ground about two fields over the road. Another fox was holloa'd close by and ran back to Heythrop and on nearly to Hook Norton where he went down the railway tunnel and was lost. A holla' from Pomfret Castle gave us short hunt to Little Tew. Then hounds went back to Heythrop where they found another fox which they hunted about the park. I came home during this. Good day. Fast run to Hook Norton.

HORSES OUT
Barney; D. Frank

DADDY AND FRANK COME DOWN ON THE FLAT.

Warm. Evenley was blank. Found an outlier between Evenley and Hinton and ran to Brackley Gorse and killed. Found at Shelswell Plantation and ran through Pitts and Mixbury Plantation to Spilsmere and Newton Purcell, back left handed by Finmere Station to Shelswell and we came home. Frank fell down crossing a grass field and nearly rolled on Daddy. Barney tried to refuse at an open ditch but was going too fast to stop and fell at the fence the other side. No harm done. Mrs Dillon got jumped off.

Mr RIGDEN AND MOUNT PART COMPANY.

HORSES OUT
Barney; D. Frank

Still and grey. A fox was found up a tree in Bletchington Park and ran very fast round the park, over the road between Kirtlington and Bletchington and on past Busby's Spinney and Hampton Poyle when he got to ground near Kidlington. Then we went back to Busby Spinney and a fox from there ran towards Northbrook but at the old cement works all trace of him was lost. Then we drew Kirtlington Park blank but a fox from Caudle ran through Weston Peat Pits and past Weston Aerodrome through Bignell Park and got to ground just the other side of the Bicester - Middleton road.

HORSES OUT
Refern; D. Hillmorton

AT THE KILL EUSTACE & Co. LUNCH COMFORTABLY.

Very still and fog nearly thick enough to stop hunting. The Brickyard and Dane Hill were blank but an outlier was found by the river between N.Aston and Deddington and ran towards N.Aston Mill on past Siretts' Farm, past the Warren, over the main road and nearly to Duns Tew, then left handed to Barton Gate, crossed the brook and then turned right handed, thru' Sandford Park, on past Conygree, past Great Tew Park and was killed in Hookerswell Farm buildings between Great Tew and Enstone. Great hunt. Hounds drew Hawk Hill and had another good run, but our horses were done, we came home.

MARGARET SCREWS UP HER COURAGE TO NO PURPOSE.

HORSES OUT
Barney; D. Hillmorton

Found at Prattle Wood and ran thru' Noke village nearly to Horton Spinney and lost. Hayne's stick heap and Weston Wood blank. Found in stick heap at Wendlebury and ran thru' Weston Wood with Weston village on right thru' Weston Peat Pits over Weston Aerodrome and lost at Middleton Stoney.

A FOX WAS DISLODGED FROM THIS TREE.

HORSES OUT
Redfern; D. Frank

Found at Longlands and ran thru' Poodle Gorse over Poundon Hill to Marsh Gibbon left handed to Marsh Gibbon station and back over Poundon Hill to Godington, left handed to Poodle and killed. Found at Stratton Copse and ran fast to Poodle from which we came home.

REDFERN AND I BREAK UP A COURTSHIP.

HORSES OUT
Redfern

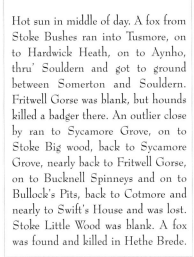

Hot sun in middle of day. A fox from Stoke Bushes ran into Tusmore, on to Hardwick Heath, on to Aynho, thru' Souldern and got to ground between Somerton and Souldern. Fritwell Gorse was blank, but hounds killed a badger there. An outlier close by ran to Sycamore Grove, on to Stoke Big wood, back to Sycamore Grove, nearly back to Fritwell Gorse, on to Bucknell Spinneys and on to Bullock's Pits, back to Cotmore and nearly to Swift's House and was lost. Stoke Little Wood was blank. A fox was found and killed in Hethe Brede.

GILBERT RECEIVES HELP

HORSES OUT
Redfern

Very hot and sunny. Bignell was blank. Drew for outliers towards Graven Hill. Found at Graven Hill and ran to Murcott, on to Merton, thru' Ambrosden and slowly towards Arncott where scent failed. A fox from Arncott Little Wood ran thru' Arncott Big Wood past Piddington and on over Muswell Hill from where I came home. Good day.

HORSES OUT

Barney

MAJOR EVANS RETRIEVES A LADY'S HORSE.

Mild and cloudy. Found at Shelswell, ran thru' Mixbury Plantation, thru' Mixbury village, under the railway on to Tingewick Woods, straight thru' these woods on to Barton Hartshorn and Hillesden, thru' Jawcott Wood and on to where he was marked to ground near Jawcott village. Wonderful hunt; best of the season. Barney went excellently. 17 miles home alone.

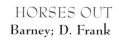

HORSES OUT
Barney; D. Frank

THE MASTER'S HORSE CAUSED A DELAY HERE.

Looked for outliers in Gubbin's Hole and then went straight to Claydon Woods. Hunted in woods till 2 and came home. 20 miles home.

STOPPED BY A WIRED UP BOTTOM

HORSES OUT
Redfern; D. Hillmorton

Found at Rowlers and ran to Rainsborough Camp and lost. Found in Rosamond's Bower and ran by Purston to Farthinghoe and Colready and killed at Hinton-in-the-Hedges.

MISS O'CONNOR IN DISTRESS

HORSES OUT
Dinah

Found at Worton Heath and ran to Barton Gate and slowly on to Glympton Heath where the hunt finished. Went back to Worton Heath and Hawk Hill but drew blank.

TOM EMBERLIN GOES IN TO SHELLSWELL FOR A DRINK.

HORSES OUT
Barney; D. Frank

Windy. Bullocks Pits blank; found at Bucknell Spinney and ran fast on Cotmore and then slowly with Stratton Audley, Brickfield and Fringford Hill on right to Brook Spinneys and Shelswell Plantation out nearly to Juniper and lost between there and Tusmore. Found in Tusmore Wood and thru' Stoke Bushes to Stoke Lyne, back to Stoke Bushes and with Hardwick on left to Hethe village and into Shelswell Plantation and lost.

HORSES OUT
Dinah; D. Hillmorton

DADDY AND HILLMORTEN WHILE HOUNDS DRAW SWAN'S NEST

Hot and sunny. Found at Whistlow Osiers and ran by Round Hill to Tinford Bridge nearly to Glympton Heath and lost near Barton. After drawing Barton Mires, Barton Bushes and Glympton Heath the rest of the day was spent in the Kiddington and Ditchley Woods.

Busby's Spinney and Ash Wood blank, found in Kirtlington Park and ran by Roundabouts to Middleton Park and lost. Found another near Chesterton and ran a ring between there and Wendlebury and lost.

GILBERT'S WARDROBE JUST LASTS OUT THE SEASON.

Gooseholme and Brackley Gorse blank. Found at Painter's and ran by the Hulls, Pitts, Mixbury and Finmere Plantations to Shelswell and lost. Found at Fringford Hill and ran fast with Stratton Copse on left to Poodle and on to Poundon where we left them still running.

Found at Swerford Park and ran towards Hook Norton right handed and to ground at Mason's Arms. Found a vixen in Happy Valley and left her. Found at Wheatfields and ran out to Lidstone.

GREAT KEENESS WAS SHOWN IN DIGGING

BUT AT THE END OF THE HOLE WAS NO CUB.

MAJOR DALY RAN NO RISKS WITH WIRE
GEORGE WAS $MADE TO NIP IT.

HORSES OUT
Dinah; D.Barney

Fine morning, turned to wet later. We found them at Dane Hill where they killed two cubs. From there they came straight to Daffodil Clump where there were three or four cubs, one of whom I believe got away and three got to ground where they were dug for without success.

HORSES OUT
Barney

MRS 'TOO SWEET' FINDS A NEW ADMIRER

IN BOB NORRIS.

Cold and blowy. Thought the meet was at 7.30 so got there well before the hounds. A cub was found and killed in Aynho Park. Another after a short run was killed in another cover. A cub from the Pits ran to Rowlers and was killed.

HORSES OUT
Barney. D.Redfern

GILBERT GREEN WITH ENVY ON SEEING DADDY

CATCH A PARTRIDGE FOR DINNER.

Soaking wet as we came home. Found at Evenley and ran over railway and Brackley sewage farm and killed at Turweston. Found in Shelswell Plantation and ran with Juniper on right and lost at Tusmore.

RELUCTANTLY CONSIDERING
WHETHER TO CONTINUE THE JUMP SEPARATELY

HORSES OUT
Barney; D. Redfern

Frosty and sunny at first. Turned to drizzel later. Motored straight to Islip from Croughton where I'd been staying. Found in Prattle Wood and ran slowly with Oddington on right and lost near Harris' Gorse. Found in Rowles Spinney and ran with Weston Wood on right and Wormough on left to railway right handed past Oddington Halt and back to Weston Wood. Very good fun. Barney not feeling like jumping today. Jumped badly and refused. Very deep going.

AT THIS OBSTACLE MISS FLEISHMANN REQUIRED HELP

HORSES OUT
Barney; D. Redfern

Found at Weston Wood after drawing the stick heap blank and ran to Oddington Halt, right handed to Harris Gorse, straight thru' to Bletchington, left handed by Hampton Poyle to Harris Gorse past Heathfield to Bletchingdton and back to Harris Gorse and killed.

LIMITED LANDING SPACE.

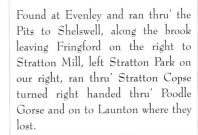

HORSES OUT
Barney

Found at Evenley and ran thru' the Pits to Shelswell, along the brook leaving Fringford on the right to Stratton Mill, left Stratton Park on our right, ran thru' Stratton Copse turned right handed thru' Poodle Gorse and on to Launton where they lost.

HORSES OUT
Barney; D.Redfern

BARNEY WAS RETURNED TO ME BY TWO

YOUNG GALLANTS.

Mild, still and dark. Found in Ambrosden village and ran to Blackthorn and on towards Marsh Gibbon left handed by Launton Station and village and left again to Marsh Gibbon, right handed to Wretchwick and lost. Got two falls. Got pushed off by a tree into a pool of water the first time. The second time didn't go fast enough at the fence and the ditch brought us down on the far side. Redfern came home lame.

BACHE HAY'S HORSE

REVERSED DOWN-STREAM.

HORSES OUT
Dinah; D. Redfern

Windy and very wet. Found in Prattle Wood and ran past Woodeaton and got to ground. An outlier on Otmoor was found in some rushes and ran into Haynes' stick heap and was bolted from there only to return later, but this time he did not succeed in getting in; however scent soon failed. Very deep going and water in all the furrows. Dinah went very well and lost a shoe in the front. Oliver Gilbey got jumped off and I caught his horse before I knew whose it was. We got home wet to the skin and very chilled, tho' when we were nearly home it cleared up into a lovely evening with a stormy sunset.

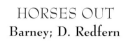

HORSES OUT
Barney; D. Redfern

THE MASTER LEADS THE HUNT AHEAD OF HOUNDS.

Mild and sunny. There were a lot of foxes in Fritwell Gorse. One was killed in the cover and another ran to Aynhoe and was lost. Returning to Fritwell Gorse another fox ran to Croughton and was lost. Stoke Big Wood was blank. So were some of the Bucknell Spinneys, but a fox from one of these ran to Ardley and was lost.

HORSES OUT
Dinah

DINAH AND I GET A LIFT HOME

Mild and windy. Prattle Wood was blank so we came back and drew Harris' Gorse blank and then went on to Busby's Spinney where a fox ran along beside the canal to the old cement works and up into Kirtlington Park, out by the lake and gave us a ringing hunt towards Weston Wood and on towards Wendlebury. Very deep going, Dinah and I got a lift back in the horse box. Not too bad a day, tho' very twisty and bad country.

HORSES OUT
Dinah; D. Barney

DINAH AND I MESS UP THE BROOK.

Rather windy and cold. Found in the Highlands and had a long ringing hunt. Hunted in the vicinity all day. It was the day of the Hunt Ball so we had the car to meet us and take us home. Dinah very lame coming home.

MRS. DILLON MAKES A FEW REMARKS ABOUT PEOPLE WHO SPLASH YOU.

Mild spring day. Drew Thenford Gardens blank. Found at Marston Ponds and ran past Keeper's Spinney on to Thenford Gorse and got to ground. Found in Cockley Brake and ran past Marston and Thenford Gorse on to ground at the Magpie.

HORSES OUT
Barney; D. Frank

LADY DILLON NEVER LACKS FOR GALLANT ASSISTANCE

Dull and cold but no wind. Found our first fox in Haine's Stick Heap and ran in a small circle and then up to Islip where he was killed in the village. We then found an outlier near the village and ran to Harris Gorse where he got to ground. We then found one in some bushes near Weston Wood which was chopped. One from Weston Wood went away over Pether's land and ran in a circle round by Charlton and leaving Oddington on the left got to ground near Harris Gorse, but was dug out and killed as was also another with him. Hounds found again in a little place near Weston-on-the-Green but could do nothing with this fox.

WE DID NOT JOIN THE BATHING PARTY.

HORSES OUT
Barney; D.Frank

Very thick fog, but the sun came thru' later. So after meeting at 12 we were able to hunt at about 12.45. Drew Piddington Wood first and a fox ran down the hill, up past Arncott Wood, away right handed over the railway towards Blackthorn, back across the railway and was lost. Arncott Little Wood was then drawn blank and we then went to Graven Hill, drawing Jasper's and the New Plantation blank on the way. A fox from Graven Hill ran a ring and back into the wood again and then out again in the same circle and was lost. Drew Chesterton blank and then hounds went home.

HORSES OUT
Barney; D. Frank

MRS. BATHURSTS MARE INTERESTS ITSELF IN AVIATION.

Found in Emberlin's kale and ran past the aerodrome along the hill side, over the Heyford - Bicester road to Northbrook where hounds lost. Found in Ballard's Firs and ran thru' Dog Kennel Copse back to Emberlin's kale and lost. Ardley was blank. Found in Stoke Big Wood but the fox got to ground at once. Another ran out Cotmore way slowly to Stratton Hall.

MRS. WOODS FOUND THE FORD ALMOST IMPRACTICABLE.

HORSES OUT
Barney; D. Frank

Found at Graven Hill, but scent was not good and after running slowly to Lower Arncott, gave out. An outlier in the meadows by Marsh Gibbon ran nearly to Launton, then round left handed in a circle and was lost near Marsh Gibbon. Poodle was next drawn blank. A fox was next found in Cotmore and ran over the main road past Stratton Audley Park, over Godington Hill and turning right handed got into a drain near Poodle.

GEN.ᴬᴸ COURAGE WAS ACCOMPANIED BY AN ARDENT FOLLOWER.

HORSES OUT
Barney

Very warm and sunny. Mrs Beaufoy gave me a lift in her horse box. Found in Piereth's Gorse and ran across the railway and parallel with it, right handed thru' Wardington leaving Edgcote just on our left nearly to Trafford Bridge and right handed back to Thorpe where he was lost. Found in Thenford Gorse and ran to Marston Ponds, left Cockley Brake just on our right, turned left over the railway just short of Steane and ran on to Halse and back left handed to Greatworth and on to Thenford Gorse. Mrs B's horse done up and we left there.

STAND BACK - GIVE THE HOUNDS ROOM PLEASE !

Stormy, turned to heavy rain and strong wind. Drew along the brook towards Hethe Brede at first but didn't find. Found in Shelswell and ran to the Pits and back and killed. Found next in Stratton Copse and ran with Chetwoode on the left and was lost near the railway when a storm came on. It was raining so hard then that the hounds went home after drawing Fringford Hill and the Brickyard blank.

COLT AND I LACK SPORTING APPRECIATION OF PARTRIDGES AT 6·30 A.M.

HORSES OUT
Colt

Rose at 5.30 and took Colt to see hounds. Windy and stormy. Colt very fresh and had to be well galloped to sober him before getting to the meet. A good many cubs were found and hunted in Glympton Heath, Barton Mires, Roundabouts and Bushes but none killed.

HORSES OUT
Frank; D. Hillmorton

UNWILLINGLY CONNECTED WITH A NOTED KICKER.

Very cold, s.w. wind, cloudy. Found in the Emberlin's orchard and ran to Upper Heyford where the fox got to ground. Found in the kale field and ran to the osier bed between Upper and Lower Heyford and killed. Found in Letchlade Gorse, ran to Middleton Ridings, right handed to Caulcott, right handed again to Upper Heyford and lost. Dog Kennel Copse and Ardley Wood blank.

HORSES OUT
Frank; D. Hillmorton

MASTER COURAGE'S PONY ELECTED TO ROLL IN THE MUD

Mild and rainy. Spent all day hunting in Bletchington, Kirtlington and Middleton Parks. Eventually a fox from Bignell ran back to Middleton Park and brought us nicely home.

ENTHUSIASTIC MEMBERS OF THE FIELD.

HORSES OUT
Frank; D. Hillmorton

North wind, very cold and incessant driving rain all day. Found in Cobbler's Pits, ran right handed thru' Rosamond's Bower, right again up to Newbottle where they checked in the wood, then left handed towards the church, back again, lost on the hill opposite Thomas Gorse. Found in Thomas Gorse ran along the bottom and up the hill to Rainsborough Camp and lost. Drew Charlton Spinneys blank and came home very wet.

HORSES OUT
Hillmorton; D. Frank

ARCHIE CUBITT DEMONSTRATED
THE FORWARD SEAT.

Mild and sunny. We spent the whole day round Weston Wood. Every time the fox got away after a short run he returned.

COLT INTRODUCED HIMSELF AND ME TO Mr HERMAN HODGE

HORSES OUT
Colt; D.Hillmortron

Cold and Bright. We arrived soon after 8 o'clock. They killed one cub in the Dean and two which they got out of a tree beyond the Dean. Rowsham Spinney had a cub but nothing could be done with it. Colt very uppish. Shall go again tomorrow.

MR HERMON HODGE
INSISTED ON THE WIDTH
OF THE ROAD BETWEEN US.

HORSES OUT
Colt; D.Hillmorton

Cold and frosty. Thick fog at first. Hunted in Worton Heath for some time, but achieved nothing and went on to Seagrove Osiers. My martingale broke and so had to go home.

MRS. WOODS WAS FIRST IN AT THE DEATH.

HORSES OUT
Frank; D. Hillmorton

Mild and Drizzly. Found and killed a fox in Evenley Park. Two foxes were found in a root field close to Evenley and were killed. A fox from Shelswell ran to the Pits and was killed. A fox from Mixbury was hunted over the railway towards Tingewick when we left.

THIS LITTLE PIG WENT A-HUNTING.

HORSES OUT
Lisnegar

Bright and sunny - turned stormy later. Rode the new horse from Frank Eldridge's. Found in Dane's Moor, ran in a circle and killed. Found in Elworth Mines and ran to ground in two fields. Found there again and killed immediately. Did not find again. Very poor day but the new horse is a lovely ride and has perfect manners.

GENERAL ALISON RAPIDLY IMITATED A TENNIS BALL.

HORSES OUT
Hillmorton; D. Frank

Very cold north wind. Found in Emberlin's Kale and ran up by the 'drome and down to the canal where he got to ground. Ran from Ballard's Firs up to Troy Farm and round pt. to pt. course and got to ground near Somerton. Found in Dog Kennel Copse and ran same line again, but lost fox. Found another near Ardley and killed him.

HORSES OUT
Lisnegar

THIS OBSTACLE PROVED DISASTROUS TO THESE JUNIORS.

Very cold wind. Showers of sleet and hail. Found outlier in tree near village and killed. Found in Haycock and gorse and ran toward Heledon and lost. Found in some gorse and got to ground. Parson's Spinney blank. Found in some gorse and ran over main road leaving Byfield on left and lost. Very poor day. No scent.

GEORGE AND CHARLES SET THE PACE COMING HOME.

HORSES OUT

Frank

Frost early, mild later. Found in Astrop Cobbler's Pits and ran back thru' the park to Thomas' Gorse, up to Rainsborough Camp, thru' Charlton and Rowlers and lost near Hinton. Found a fox near Brackley Gorse and ran nearly to Halse and got to ground. Cockley Brake and Thenford Gorse blank. Found in Piereth's Gorse and got to ground in a few fields. Long ride home.

HORSES OUT
Frank; D. Hillmorton

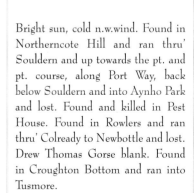

SIR NORMAN HOPED HIS HORSE WOULD GET
ITS BACK DOWN BEFORE IT WAS RETURNED
TO HIM

Bright sun, cold n.w.wind. Found in Northerncote Hill and ran thru' Souldern and up towards the pt. and pt. course, along Port Way, back below Souldern and into Aynho Park and lost. Found and killed in Pest House. Found in Rowlers and ran thru' Colready to Newbottle and lost. Drew Thomas Gorse blank. Found in Croughton Bottom and ran into Tusmore.

PUSS WENT WHILE THE GOING WAS GOOD.

HORSES OUT
Frank; D. Hillmorton

Very cold. Snow drifts round the fences. Found in the kale field and killed down by the railway. Found in the osier bed and ran to Middleton and on by Northbrook to ground near Lower Heyford. Found in Dog Kennel Copse and ran to Letchlade Gorse and round by Middleton ridings back to Dog Kennel and killed. Found in Fritwell Gorse and ran to Somerton and got to ground above the railway tunnel.

HORSES OUT
Marigold; D.Shorty

Cold and cloudy, very big crowd of foot people. Took two hours to find a fox, but eventually found and had quite a nice hunt finishing at Poodle Gorse.

THE BOTTOM OF THE HILL CAME FAR TOO QUICKLY FOR HIS LIKING.

Rather cold and cloudy. Drizzled later. Found in Graven Hill Wood and ran thru' Ambrosden to Arncott Wood and on to Muswell Hill where the field was held up on forbidden land and hounds ran on towards Piddington.

INTREPID BAREBACK RIDER.

HORSES OUT
Lisnegar; D. Shorty

No foxes in Dashwood's Gorse, but three were killed in the gorse on the Hempton side of the brook. One fox was found and killed on Ilbury Hill in the gorse. One fox was killed in Hawk Hill.

JOHN DEWAR HARRISON AND HIS HORSE SHIED AT HAVING THEIR PHOTOGRAPH TAKEN.

HORSES OUT
Marigold; D. Shorty

Opening meet. Stratton Copse was blank. An outlier from Fringford Hill ran into Fringford village and was lost. Poodle Gorse was blank. An outlier near Poundon ran back to Poodle and was lost. Cotmore was blank. Very bad outlook for season with Stratton Copse, Poodle and Cotmore all blank so early.

LUCA'S PONY GOT BEATEN BY ALL WHO PASSED.

HORSES OUT
Marigold; D. Shorty

Mild and stormy. Found at Glympton Heath and ran to Barton Roundhill, back to Steeple Barton and back to the Mines and lost. Barton Bushes were blank. A fox from a kale field at Whistlow ran to Steeple Barton and back to the Roundhill and up over the main road to Rousham and was lost. An outlier in the rushy meadows by Haydon ran towards North Aston and on to the Fox Inn and was lost.

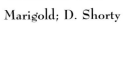

HORSES OUT
Marigold; D. Shorty

SHE WAS RESCUED BY COL. BLACKER

DADDY HELD HIS HORSE

Found in Middleton Home Wood after drawing Kirtlington Roundabouts and Cocked Hat Wood blank, ran across Weston Aerodrome and on to Wormough and back to Rignell and lost.

DEDDINGTON BROOK CAUSED CHAOS.

MAJOR FLEMING , COL. BALLAD. J. BLETSOE.

HORSES OUT
Lisnegar; D. Peter

Found in Sirett's Osiers and ran up around Godwin's farm and back to N.Aston where he got to ground close to where he had been found. Found a fox in Godwin's kale and ran over Bowman's Bridge and along the brook and up thru' N.Aston and down towards the river where he was marked to ground near N.Aston Mill. We drew Millington's blank, but found in Dashwood's gorse and ran over the brook and got to ground in the brick yard near Deddington.

THE MENACE

(LITTLE MISS ONEROD)

Rather raw and cloudy. Poor's Piece and Fritwell Gorse were blank. a fox from Stoke Big Wood ran to Ardley and was lost. Stoke Little Wood was blank. A fox from Col. Blacker's drain ran a few fields and got killed in the Bucknell Spinneys. A fox was holloa'd from Caversfield and ran thru' Bullocks Pits and back parallel with the main Buckinghamshire road, past Cotmore and got to ground in a hayrick nearby.

DADDY AND PETER, OVER-EXCITED AT THE PROSPECT OF JUMPING. LOST THEIR EQUILIBRIUM.

HORSES OUT
Marigold; D. Peter

High winds, cold and cloudy. Found at Rignell and ran very fast to Buttermilk Gorse and got to ground. Found two on Ilbury Hill, one got to ground immediately and the other was chopped. Dashwood Gorse was blank. A fox from Worton Heath ran fast to Duns Tew, on past Dashwood's Gorse towards the brook then turned back up the hill to "The Fox" and checked.

LANGA LANGA BUYS EXPENSIVE STEEPLECHASERS
TO ESCAPE FROM MRS. _____

HORSES OUT
Marigold

Mild and cloudy. Drew for outliers down by Hampton Poyle, but found none. Found in Harris Gorse and ran to Black Leys, turned right back to Heathfield and on to Weston Wood and back to Harris Gorse where he got to ground. Ash Wood and Baker's Copse were blank. A fox from the Caudle ran up towards the Roundabout, but turned back towards Weston Peat Pits and ran on to Weston Wood and up to Islip and back to Weston Wood.

MARIGOLD AND I ENTICED POOR MR PARSONS TO · HIS DOWNFALL.

HORSES OUT
Marigold

Bold s. wind. Bright and cloudy at intervals. Millingtons Gorse was blank. A fox from Dane Hill crossed the brook and ran down the valley, turning right handed up past Godwins to the gardens at N.Aston where he was hunted about in the shrubs and eventually got to ground in Sirett's Osiers. Another fox sprang up suddenly in the boundary fence and got to ground immediately. A fox from Dashwood's Gorse ran up to Duns Tew, hid in a rick yard, was eventually discovered and ran towards Worton Heath, turned back towards Barton and was lost.

HORSES OUT
Marigold; D. Shorty

MY LORD JUSTICE ROCHE'S HORSE HAD NO RESPECT FOR THE LAW.

Still and misty. Drew all the Ditchley and Kiddington Covers blank. Found at Glympton heath and ran in a short circle back to the cover and then ran fast to Steeple Barton where the fox was killed. Barton Bushes was blank, but Barton Mires held a fox who ran down the valley to Purgatory.